I0463552

5S Office Management

By Ade Asefeso MCIPS MBA

First Edition

ISBN-13: 978-1500994679

ISBN-10: 1500994677

Publisher: AA Global Sourcing Ltd
Website: http://www.aaglobalsourcing.com

Table of Contents

Disclaimer

This publication is designed to provide competent and reliable information regarding the subject matter covered. However, it is sold with the understanding that the author and publisher are not engaged in rendering professional advice. The authors and publishers specifically disclaim any liability that is incurred from the use or application of contents of this book.

If you purchased this book without a cover you should be aware that this book may have been stolen property and reported as "unsold and destroyed" to the publisher. In this case neither the author nor the publisher has received any payment for this "stripped book."

Dedication

This book is to my family and friends who seems to have been sent here to teach me something about who I am supposed to be. They have nurtured me, challenged me, and even opposed me.... But at every juncture has taught me!

This book is dedicated to my lovely boys, Thomas, Michael and Karl. Teaching them to manage their finance will give them the lives they deserve. They have taught me more about life, presence, and energy management than anything I have done in my life.

Chapter 1: Introduction

When was the last time you saw your desktop? If your answer is, "Hmm...I don't really remember," do you realize how much time and energy you are wasting just looking for stuff? I'm guessing that you already know you are wasting time. Or maybe you are so embarrassed by your messy office that you don't even let clients see it. You end up meeting with clients in a conference room. You did like to get your office cleaned up, but you have no idea where to start.

Let me suggest a concept called: 5S. 5S is an organizational tool born out of the Toyota production system called Lean.

What is 5S?

5S is a basic, fundamental, systematic approach for productivity, quality and safety improvement in all types of business.

A 5S (Five S) program is usually a part of, and the key component of establishing a Visual Workplace and are both a part of Kaizen; a system of continual improvement; which is a component of lean manufacturing.

The 5S program focuses on:
1. Having visual order.
2. Organization.
3. Cleanliness.
4. Standardization.

The results you can expect from a 5S program are:
1. Improved profitability.
2. Efficiency.
3. Service and safety.

The principles underlying a 5S program at first appear to be simple, obvious common sense and they are; but until the advent of 5S programs many businesses ignored these basic principles.

What is Lean?

The core idea of Lean is to maximize customer value while minimizing waste. Simply put, Lean means creating more value for customers with fewer resources. A Lean organization understands customer value and focuses its key processes to continuously increase it.

The basic idea behind 5S office management is that a messy office is full of waste. Not only the waste you can see, i.e. the mess; but the time wasted in looking for the right file, your phone, eye glasses. You get the idea. (Caveat: Lean tools like 5S are designed to work together to create a synergistic whole. Ideally, they should not be implemented individually, but rather as a part of an entire Lean organization. That being said, 5S is something you can implement today, with the understanding that your goal is to create a more effective and efficient office as a whole.)

The 5S System

Sort: Step one is to gather all your stuff into groups: Files, letters, sticky notes, pens, legal pads, paper clips, etc.

Straighten: Here is where my mom's old saying, "A place for everything and everything in its place," comes to mind. Organize your office so that everything has a spot. For example, your pens are always in a certain spot, your legal pads are in a certain spot, your sticky notes are always in a certain spot. My guess is you already do this with two items in your office; your inbox and your outbox. They are in the same spot on your desk that they have always been. Imagine how frustrating it would be if they moved around and you never knew where they were on a given day.

Shine: Now that you have sorted and straightened it is time to clean things up. Polish and clean your office. Take the time to do this. You will feel great when you are done, and your staff will wonder what is come over you. Once you have set the example, you can plan a 5S day for the whole office. Make it a party. Bring in pizza and make it fun. The first person to 5S their space and keep it that way for a week, two weeks, a month, gets a gift card to their favourite restaurant!

Standardize: Standardization in a manufacturing setting (i.e. a Toyota plant) is about creating an environment in which, for example, workers don't waste time looking for tools. In your office it means

9

developing a consistently organized office for you and your staff.

Sustain: Finally, you have got to create a system to maintain the order you have created. In other words, you have got to make it a habit. Spend just five minutes at the end of each day making sure everything is where it's supposed to be. Do this every day for a few weeks and it will become automatic. You won't be able to leave your office until you have tidied it up.

Chapter 2: Why 5S is Necessity in Today's Busy Office Environment

One of the first tools everyone seems to jump to is 5S. Lets implement 5S to start our lean journey, whether that is the right answer for them or not. On the manufacturing floor, 5S is more straight forward. Employees may not like it at first but 5S has an easier time getting accept on the manufacturing floor.

The flip side is in the office. 5S is very applicable in the office but harder to apply appropriately. I can't count how many times I have heard, "You aren't taking my pictures away from me." or "It is stupid to label my phone and stapler. I know where they are and where they go." Who am I to argue? I totally agree and would feel the same way.

When I stopped to think about it, people felt this way because of the improper understanding and/or execution of 5S in the office. Most likely someone came in and dictated how they were going to clean up their area and label everything and they would be graded on it.

That is not the intent of 5S. It is to quickly surface problems so they can be recognized and addressed.

So when and how does someone apply 5S to the office appropriately? The first answer is when it is a shared space. If someone else will have to use the same area or desk to do the same or similar work, then this is a place that 5S can help. Just like the manufacturing floor someone can come in and spend too much time re-arranging the desk area for their work or spend too much time looking for something that is out of place. Unlike your own personal desk that no one else will use. If no one else will use it, then why label, because you know where everything is. Even "messy" people have a system so leave it be.

A company that I visited recently did a great job of applying 5S to the office. The work was processing layouts through a computer system. People had their own desk, but could have to share it with others. So if Mike left on vacation, Maureen would come to his desk to do that work, because no matter what the layouts had to be processed that day. So they standardized the colour of the folders for "To Be Done", "In Process", and "Completed". They standardized what drawer the folder went into when completed and how the work area was laid out for the work. The work area was the computer and the things directly around it to get the job done. They also standardized where their visual signal for needing the next job was on the desk so no one had to search for it. The rest of the area was for Mike to personalize with his pictures, calendars, and what not. It did not interfere with the work that was needed to be done.

The group become more efficient and standardized without losing any personalization because of this, for 2 years this worked very well and there was ownership. The only reason it isn't around now is because of new technology that eliminated that work. The challenge is to know when and how to use 5S, especially in the office.

More than sixty years ago Toyota created the 5S system, a method of organizing and maintaining neat and clutter-free manufacturing facilities that encouraged productivity. Today, manufacturing plants and offices world-wide have implemented the philosophies and practices of the TPS (Toyota Production System).

Lean Office principles of 5S may seem mysterious at first, but are quite sensible when focusing on each one individually. After 5S-ing the office and committing to keeping it in place, you will be able to concentrate on the tasks at hand more easily, and productivity will increase.

Let's take a look at the 5S' and see why they are a necessity in today's busy office environment.

1. Sort

Scenario: As you look around your office, you notice the items that have been tucked under your desk, piled on top of a filing cabinet or inherited from a previous employee when you began your job three years ago. Even though you have never needed these items, you still have them. It's time to implement the first S - Sort.

Begin by considering: What do I need to do my job everyday? Think of your office as expensive real estate. Only items that add value to your daily routines and tasks deserve to sit on your desk and take up space. When in doubt, move it out. (Or, in the environmentally-conscious spirit of recycling, give it to someone who needs it!)

Application: Conducting a sort/purge of filing drawers and hard drives will free up much-needed space. Reviewing your company's retention policy before starting this process helps you to make quicker decisions and gives you permission to either hang on to an item or release it. To help speed up the Sort process, have a large trash can and shredding bin available.

2. Straighten/Set-In-Order

Scenario: You have just been handed a new project and your boss suggests a similar proposal which you worked on a year ago for another client. You open up your hard drive files and within sixty seconds, you are reviewing the previous file. It feels great to be able to locate an older document without having to spend hours looking for it.

Straighten up your area by creating specific "homes" for files, objects and equipment. You will use things more often and easily put them away when they are designated to a specific location.

Application: We have all seen pictures of a workbench pegboard with outline drawings for each tool. This is a prime example of Straightening and Setting in Order. You can do the same with the office supplies on your desk. Using electrical tape (available in several colours) create an outline on your desk for your stapler, 3-hold punch, phone, laptop, and other desk accessories. Instantly, you will be able to see if something is missing or out of order.

Using labels will help in the Straightening process too. You can apply them to individual shelves, cabinets, and drawers in your office. They will act as visual reminders of what goes where and help keep you from stashing items where they don't belong.

3. Shine/Sweep

Toyota discovered that maintaining the equipment and deep cleaning the facilities decreased the number of breakdowns and the cost of repairs. A clean environment encourages organization and also is an attitude-booster.

Scenario: You need to retrieve something from the dreaded storage room. The last time you were there, it took an hour to uncover what you were looking for in the dusty, cluttered mess. Thanks to 5S, when you flip on the light switch, you discover that someone has already cleaned and organized to help this space undergo a major transformation. Ahhh, life is simple/pleasures.

Application: Once a week (I like to do it on Fridays), wipe off flat surfaces such as desktops, filing cabinets and book shelves with a damp paper towel, cleaning

15

cloth or disinfectant wipes. Talk to your IT department about their preferences for cleaning your keyboard and monitor. Use a can of air to deal with the dust bunnies hiding amongst the cords behind your computer and under your desk. Your equipment will run better, and you will breathe easier in a clean, dust-free office.

4. Standardize

Bringing standardization into the office allows for systems to be put in place so everyone follows procedures the same way. This might mean creating a form used for inbound customer service calls, creating a colour-coded filing system or using a checklist before sending product to the customer. Standardizing processes and procedures lowers the error rate (referred to as Waste of Defects) and ensures that 5S techniques will be applied.

Scenario: Several individuals in your department handle inquiry calls for new business. Your job is to follow up on the initial calls once leads have been qualified; however, the format of the information that you receive varies by who handled the call.

Application: Develop a standardized form (electronically or paper) for all initial inquiries to ensure that complete and thorough information will appear in the same format every time. Standardizing any process will cut down on errors (Waste of Defects) and increase productivity.

5. Sustain

We do not live in a paperless society yet, and the paper trail often leads to your desk. Paper, projects and "stuff" are constantly streaming into our offices so we must be proactive in returning items to their designated areas (straightening) and developing processes for handling incoming information and projects (standardization). After developing a daily routine of Sort, Straighten, Sweep and Standardize, the final 5S step of Sustain will occur more naturally.

Application: Just keep it up! Fight the urge to put things away tomorrow. Make a checklist as a reminder to sustain all of your new good habits. Check the list at the end of everyday, or at least at the end of every week.

6. Safety

Many companies have added a sixth "S" – Safety. While this topic is common in manufacturing settings, it isn't considered a very relevant topic in the office. But safety issues always exist and are worth our attention. Obviously, any accident; whether on the manufacturing floor or in the office costs the company money in lost labour and health benefits, and costs the employees in pain and lost salary.

Injuries related to tripping over loose cords, tangled cables or piles of stuff being stored on the floor is easily fixed. Also, if your desk surface is so full of papers, stacks and stuff, you may be using your lap as a work surface, putting yourself at risk for strained neck and shoulder muscles. Addressing the well-being of employees will enhance the other S's and improve quality of work. Always put Safety first. The dividends are too high to ignore.

Application: Wrapping up this "S" is easy. Use bag ties or wire ties to keep cords from becoming tangled. Staple "snaky" cords to the baseboards, and file those piles away each day. Approaching your office with 5S in mind will eventually become second nature. Soon you will find yourself sorting and straightening things at home and spotting areas that could be improved with a little standardization.

Chapter 3: Why 5S Does Not Work in the office

In this chapter I will explain why 5S does not work in the office based on my own thinking and experience with it over the years. For those of you unfamiliar with 5S it is a lean tool associated with workplace organization. In fact, 5S is an abbreviation for 5 Japanese words: seiri, seiton, seiso, seiketsu and shitsuke. These are often translated into English equivalents such as sorting (removing unnecessary items from the workplace), straightening (making sure every item remaining has a proper place), shine (actual cleaning, e.g. with paper towels), standardization (making the previous 3 systematic), and sustain (keeping it going).

Companies spend a lot of money to implement this system in production in order to lay the groundwork for other lean tools such as TPM and SMED. They rightfully believe that an organized workplace is the foundation of further improvement. In fact, any organized workplace is better than an unorganized one, as the two causes of quality issues in manufacturing (mistakes and excessive variation) are influenced by the amount of organization present in the manufacturing area.

Due to its popularity and the fact that it does lead to more organized workplaces when implemented properly, at some point someone believed that it would be good to implement 5S in the office and thus another misapplication of an otherwise okay lean tool commenced. Today, in many companies, you will see people who patiently explain to visitors how office 5S has led to greater organization, cost savings, and other magical effects believed by executives of companies who should know better. The reality is that when an office 5S program is implemented there is usually a training done followed by some cleaning and organizing and then someone (or a team) gets to do the 5S audits in the office. See, you can't effectively manage something unless you can measure it (I write that with tongue firmly planted in cheek as that thinking is some of the most damaging in all of business). People with clipboards walk around and harass office workers while thoughtfully examining their desks, checking that their staplers are within the taped marks, and even in some cases opening desk drawers and counting how many ink pens are inside.

All in the name of improvement. For those keeping score, or whose bonus relies on the numbers, and those in upper management who don't know better, these activities are part and parcel with the magical improvements expected by simply applying an okay idea in another part of the business. For the rest of the people it is an amusing distraction at best and an absolutely boorish waste of time at worst. I know this because I have been on both sides of the 5S audit equation, as the auditee and as the auditor. I can honestly say that I don't know which side is worse.

5S as a tool for organizing a manufacturing workplace is an okay idea in that it is simply a little bit of structured "common sense". The people who work in manufacturing; the operators, technicians, and supervisors can see the limited value such organization brings and usually don't have a problem with it. The silly audits that must accompany such initiatives (otherwise, how does management know that the lean guys are doing their jobs?) are a necessary evil to achieve a modicum of cleanliness and organization. Here is the main point, for a repetitive operation and/or one that relies on closely following detailed work instructions having a clean and well-organized workplace can lead to reduced mistakes and variation, inevitably leading to better quality; however, such repetitive operations do not typically exist in the office, hence the lack of value of 5S there. Let me elaborate....

Imagine that you are a Production Manager in a factory with a few hundred people and around $100 million in annual sales volume. Your typical day might consist of a morning meeting with your team followed by spending several hours on the manufacturing floor to see what happened in the past day and examine the various operations. You may have a meeting with the Controller to review the month's production volume and the Safety Manager to better understand a new ordinance drafted by the local government. You grab a quick lunch, double-check your emails, talk for a few minutes with the Plant Manager then head back out to the manufacturing floor to see what is happening at the start of second shift. You may discover that a relatively important piece of equipment has broken down and you work with the Quality Manager to arrange the appropriate process deviation

21

documentation as well as the Engineering Manager to arrange for alternate machinery. Finally you end the day with a short meeting about next year's performance rating system with the HR Manager before heading home a little bit after dark. You have put in a more than 10 hours today and gird yourself to do more of the same tomorrow.

At no time during your day did it matter at all that the stapler on your desk was within the little yellow tape lines or that you had exactly 3 ink pens in your desk drawer. Such a dynamic and fluid role is not helped at all by delineating required markings on a desk and specific locations for this book or that filing cabinet. Seeing the results of the latest office 5S audits posted on the bulletin board doesn't even register. For people with this kind of work, office 5S falls in the boorish waste of time category very quickly. They are doing the kind of work that is almost the opposite of repetitive and it is not helped one bit by some program to put little tape lines on people's desks and count how many ink pens are in their drawers. Of course the Production Manager's activities must fall within some kind of system, and that is why we have ISO 9001 and other management system standards, but applying a concept intended for the manufacturing area into such a working environment is actually damaging to these people who conduct key activities to keep the business running.

On the other hand if 5S System is used to reorganize your office rather than just your desk and drawer it will work and yield benefits.

Chapter 4: 5S System Challenges

You will face many challenges implementing and sustaining a 5S System. One of those is that a 5S System represents change. One way to make the change easy for employees is to use a slow and steady method of implementation.

The first thing to remember is there is no cookie cutter solution when it comes to developing and implementing a 5S System. Each organization is different as are the people who work in them. You must examine how your organization works and tailor your 5S System to fit.

For a 5S System to be successful you must be successful at changing the culture and the behaviour of employees and management. Since by nature people are resistant to change this can be the biggest obstacle to overcome. By using the slow and steady approach you will be able to gradually change the culture.

The key is to start small and never stop improving. By using the Kaizen approach of small incremental changes it allows your employees to adapt to the changes with little disruption. With this type of implementation the 5S System will be better received and be more sustainable.

One Small Step at a Time

Start with one area of the office, department or other area you want to implement a 5S System in. Then gradually work your way through the organization step by step. This makes it much easier to plan for and implement. You are working with smaller groups so education about 5S is less of a burden. Once you have that area squared away and running under a sustainable 5S System move on to the next one.

Be sure that before you move to the next area you have put in place a system to sustain the 5S System. You don't want to go in, implement the 5S System and move on to the next area. Be sure you have properly trained and followed up with the employees in this area before you move on to the next.

Your first 5S System implementation should be your best. It will be the showcase of how much better the work environment is. Consider it your training ground for building your 5S System. Learn what works and what does not. This will help you avoid mistakes when you move on to other areas and improve your 5S System.

A successful implementation of a 5S System in your first area will show the rest of the organization that there is nothing to fear. Once they see how much better the sustained 5S area is and how well the employees like it, it will make it much more acceptable as you move on.

Get Managers and Supervisors Onboard

Spend a lot of time with your managers and supervisors. Educate them on 5S and get them onboard early. They will be the ones who will help sustain the 5S System and can give you valuable insight into how it will best work in their area.

A 5S System is change and change is often met with resistance. By starting small you avoid the overwhelming effect that some may feel. For many organizations, particularly large ones this slow and steady approach works best.

Chapter 5: 8 Classic Office Wastes

In the office environment, the 8 classic waste types of the Lean methodology manifest in different ways than we see on the factory floor. Learn to identify waste in the office so you can eliminate it and improve your business performance and your work environment.

In the Lean methodology, there are generally 8 categories of waste we learn to look for and eliminate. For the most part, we all learn to identify and reduce these wastes in workspaces such as factory floors, assembly lines, test laboratories, or hospital rooms.

Next, if we are progressive, we will reduce waste in highly repeatable business processes such as taking orders from customers, delivering reports to customers or regulatory agencies, and other processes where it is easy to both map and measure the process and its waste. What about the other office programs, ones that aren't so easy to map or measure? Can't we get the waste out of them too?

It might be less straightforward to identify and remove waste from processes that drive projects, or that are used during projects, but it can, and should be done. A challenge that must be overcome, however, is learning how to identify the waste in the office.

On the factory or workroom floor, we learned to look for the waste. It is most obvious in the following forms, which are easy clues that a process is not performing efficiently.

Inventory: Parts stacked up before, in, or at the end of a process is a waste by itself, but also a manifestation of other wastes such as transportation, defects, and overproduction.

Motion: People moving around a lot is a waste and also a manifestation of over processing or transportation.

In short we quickly learn to spot inventory and motion as two key indicators of waste.

What about at your desk in the office? You know the waste is there. You feel it. It's harder to see, though. The reason is that your workspace is inside your computer. Inventory exists, but it's in your e-mail box, not on your desktop. Motion takes place, but it's not in the hallways, it's also inside your computer network.

To identify and eliminate the waste that plagues your office, learn to identify the 8 wastes in their digital, virtual manifestations. Here is a list of the 8 common wastes of Lean, and some ideas about how they manifest in the office environment.

1. Transportation: Movement of the work. Manifestations include handoffs where the work is transferred from one person to another.

28

Transportation of electronic files is particularly insidious because it frequently results in multiple, varying copies of the work, which must eventually be reconciled. It leads to other wastes such as defects, overproduction, and processing. Transportation is also an opportunity for a defect when the work goes to the wrong person or fails to get to the right person.

2. Inventory: Work that is waiting to be processed. Inventory is a common result of multi-tasking and otherwise un-balanced workloads. Inventory can be found in e-mail or work order in-boxes, to-do lists, product development pipelines, and resource assignment charts. If a person has three tasks to complete, it is guaranteed that two of them are waiting (in inventory) while that person performs the third. If you want to be able to see inventory like you do on the factory floor, you must make the lists, in-boxes, resource assignments, and project pipelines visible in your workspace.

3. Motion: People moving or working without producing. Meetings are motion in the sense that they are work without producing, unless a decision is made or information is produced during the meeting. The motion you see of people moving from conference room to conference room and back to their desks is indeed wasted motion, but it is probably not the waste to target first. Motion shows up as people search for files they can't find, in phone calls to track down information, or from unnecessary button clicks to get to the bottom of a work order to update the to-do list. Most un-productive work takes place inside the electronic system while the person is sitting at his/her desk or while they are sitting in a meeting.

4. Waiting: People waiting for information in order to do work. This is another common result of multi-tasking, and also the primary cause of multi-tasking. People work on other things while they wait for one thing to be processed and made ready. Unfortunately, when the one thing finally becomes ready, we tend to finish what we started before getting back to it; because of multi-tasking, waiting is difficult to observe. You must ask questions to discover it, or identify it yourself when you run into it. It's perhaps the most common and wasteful waste of them all in the office.

5. Overproduction: Producing unnecessary work or deliverables. Overproduction shows up in multiple copies of information, producing reports that aren't read, writing formal documents or content where only the table is read, reply all, working on deliverables that aren't important, and delivering the same information in multiple deliverables or formats. Overproduction frequently shows up when managers ask underlings to do things that make the manager's life easier.

6. Over Processing: Unnecessary effort to get the work done. Over Processing shows up in additional signature approvals, data entry or data format changes, frequently revising documents or information, or complex forms or databases that require information to be entered repeatedly. Over Processing often results from the creation of multiple versions of a piece of work, that now must be reconciled into the true work.

7. Defects: Any work that did not accomplish its purpose or was not correct the first time. Defects include late work, incorrect information, conflicting information, instructions that must be clarified, insufficient information, partially complete work or information, miss-named files, lost files or information, and anything that must be reworked. Rework is the pain that results from defects. Find the re-work and you will find the Defect waste.

8. Underutilized Skills and Ideas: Capabilities of people that are not used or leveraged. This happens frequently in large organizations where the skills and backgrounds of everyone are not common knowledge. This can vary from not capturing ideas that employees might have for new products or innovations, to the six-figure salary executive correcting data entry errors in a financial spreadsheet. The biggest crime in this category is not empowering or enabling the people most intimate with a process to improve the process.

Hopefully, the short descriptions above give you some translation between wastes on factory, assembly, or laboratory spaces, and the virtual workspace of the office environment. Look around. Observe the work you do today and see how much work is in your inventory waiting for you to get around to it, and how often you are waiting for someone or something in order to get started.

Here is the big one. Do your meetings produce value by producing new information or making decisions, or do they fall in the category of waste? If you are sitting around sharing existing information, then the meeting is waste. Sharing information may be necessary and important, but is there a less time-consuming way to achieve the same result?

It is difficult to see the waste in the office, but we know it's there because we can feel it. My best advice for finding and eliminating waste in the office is to chase the pain. Hunt down the rework, the overtime, the stress and frustration, and you will quickly begin putting your fingers on the waste and its causes.

Address the causes of the waste. Eliminate them. In doing so, you will not only make your business more productive, but it will be a much less painful place to work.

Chapter 6: Areas of Waste Inventory in the Office

Waste of Inventory, as defined by the Toyota Production System, is easier to spot in a manufacturing setting than in an office. Be assured, though, it's there! Waste in a plant is usually quite visible. On the surface it is easy to see raw materials and resources that are not being used . Piles of sheet metal and other parts sitting around are easy to spot too. But in an office, waste can be a little trickier to see and identify.

1. Processes: Think about the number of signatures required to get an initiative approved and in place in your company. How long does the paperwork sit in someone's office? Sometimes a bottleneck occurs which keeps things from moving forward. If this is the case, can a few signatures be removed from the layers presently required? Setting egos aside and putting the customer first will allow for processes to be streamlined.

2. Customer orders: Once someone places an order with your company, how long do they wait until it is fulfilled and shipped? This represents another process that needs to be studied and evaluated on a regular basis to make sure that the customer's needs are being met.

3. Paper: Paper represents one of the most common wastes in an office. Are you hanging on to items because you are not sure whether or not they need to be saved? Reviewing your company's retention policies will give you the freedom to either keep or throw the paper that surrounds you. Start today and start out small. Each day moving forward give yourself 10 minutes to open a drawer, remove two of papers/files and see how much can be released. You will probably be amazed at what can be released as well as the amount of drawer space you gain.

4. **Filing Cabinets:** Some years ago I was consulting with a senior level manager at a local hospital. She had 20 filing drawers in her small office. That is 4 five-drawer filing cabinets. After sorting and purging the contents, she was left with 5 drawers of records which she was required to keep. 15 drawers of papers were shredded and recycled and once the three empty filing cabinets were removed, it looked like an entirely new office with enough space to add a small table and chairs.

5. **Office Supplies:** Having too many office supplies isn't as easy to spot as you did think. Sometimes people become mini "hoarders" in keeping their favourite pens and sticky notes tucked away. I confess. I love office supplies and based on what I have observed in others' offices, I am not alone. What if your employer declared a moratorium on the purchasing of supplies? Would you freak out? I know of a company who did just this. It took nearly six months for the employees to completely use up the supplies that were tucked into the recesses of the company. To avoid this Waste of Inventory, designate

one person in each department to oversee the purchasing and maintenance of office supplies.

6. Time: It is something we all have equal shares of yet sometimes we feel as if we are being shorted on our daily allotment of 24 hours. Identifying wasted time is hard to do because we don't always want to admit that we are wasteful in this area. At the office, do you spend too much time in meetings or being interrupted by others? How about the amount of time spent reading and processing emails? If you are checking email more than 3-4 times a day, you have got room for improvement. Using a time log sheet or software will help you to be more realistic in understanding where your time is being spent and see where adjustments need to be made.

Discovering wasteful areas in and around your office will hopefully motivate you to remove that waste and replace it with more efficient systems and processes.

Chapter 7: Removing Office Waste

Nothing can stir up a group of placid professionals like informing them that those time-saving principles of workplace organization known as 5S will be coming soon to their office. Even among die-hard lean thinkers there is an alarming number who think that 5S "can't be done" in the office to any similar degree that they do it in a factory, warehouse or even the retail floor. Perhaps it is something in the carpet.

I have seen 5S in the office with both laudable and laughable results. The difference is largely in the attitude of the people. Either they are making 5S work for them, or 5S is making them work. Rather than discuss 5S in any depth, let's assume that the people leading 5S have done their homework and have a good understanding of what it is and isn't.

Although 5S is the place many organizations start in applying lean principles and tools, there can be some initial resistance from office people due to its manufacturing heritage. In the office we work with information and not things after all, so what does "sort and straighten" really mean? People are often surprised at how much stuff there is in the office and how the disorganization of this stuff affects the quality of their work, productivity and even job satisfaction. Just watch people do their work, time it and look for the non-productive bits. So the first guideline is to gain agreement on waste removal.

There is clearly something to this resistance to office 5S. Process is process and waste is everywhere. Very few office workers would say that their processes are waste-free or that there are no problems which need to be solved. Those few who say this are experiencing a failure to communicate, are delusional or are lying to maintain the status quo. I have worked through all three. Each requires a different sort of intervention before even attempting to talk about 5S. Once that is done, the first step is to gain an unwavering agreement that waste exists, categorize and name them, and develop motivation to remove these waste. Put the customer first, team members next, and then quality and cost metrics after that. Once that is done 5S becomes one of several means to the end of waste removal, often the simplest and most convenient means. Rarely does 5S fail to address at least some of the root causes of problems in the office; however, be pragmatic and change course and use whatever tool you need to solve the problem rather than insisting on 5S. Having said that, from the point of view of promoting 5S successfully in the early stages, the second guideline is to look for the nail.

When you have a hammer and you know there are nails about, it's not always bad to go looking for the nails. Nails can be trip hazards and should be hammered in to shore up the structure in any case. But the expression "hammer looking for a nail" exists because well-intentioned people learn about improvement systems such as the 5S and try prescriptively deploy it across the board without understanding the original intent of the tool, or the unique characteristics of the workplace in which to apply it. In short, if you are on the path to office 5S then look for motion waste. Time searching for information is waste. Time rearranging information or stuff is waste. Clicking through multiple screens on the computer is waste. Focus on quick and accurate retrieval of files, data, tools or anything required to get the job done properly. Make it easy to retrieve any bit of information in less than 30 seconds. Once the usefulness of 5S has been demonstrated in one specific way, it becomes easier to expand the application of 5S towards reducing errors, waiting and other wastes.

As a side-note, sorting, the first S, can have a large positive impact on available office space. This space savings aspect of office 5S has been largely overlooked. The main reason for this may be the fact that it is harder to convert open office space into useful space, while open production space can be used for more value-added output. On a per square foot basis, there are also more walls and monuments in an office than in the typical factory. People in the office also tend to personalize and root themselves to space in the office in many Western companies in a way that is almost unhealthy. This brings us to the topic of culture and its effect on how to deploy 5S in the office, and our second guideline. Whenever we attempt to adapt kaizen techniques beyond their place of origin (the shop floor) we need to go to the new environment to study the natives.

Those of us who have lived overseas among the natives of those cultures, or those of us who work with multinational teams have some understanding that people are different, and beg to be understood. Even those of us who live in the least culturally diverse and most racially and linguistically uniform communities are fooling ourselves if we think our workplace is a monoculture. We will find that in fact we all work within a multicultural environment. People are people, but there are different cultures between the shop floor, the office, the sales force in the field, and those who work among mahogany walls. If you want to be a missionary of your ideas to these different tribes and cultures you need to learn their language and customs.

We shall look at three levels of culture below.

1. The Concrete: The most visible and tangible level of culture which includes the most surface-level things like clothes, music, food, games, etc. These parts of culture are often provide the focus for multicultural "festivals" or "celebrations."

2. The Behavioural: How we define our social roles, the language we speak, and our approaches to nonverbal communication. The Behavioural level is a reflection of values. This includes language, gender roles, family structure, political affiliation, and other items that situation us organizationally in society.

3. The Symbolic: This includes our values and beliefs. It can be abstract but it is most often the key to how individuals define themselves. It includes values systems, customs, spirituality, religion, worldview, beliefs, mores, etc.

So what does this all mean in terms of doing 5S in the office? Any workplace can and should be understood from a cultural perspective, but the office needs to be seen as a second culture, that which makes an organization immediately multicultural. The office is many times more of a clear reflection of the culture of the people working there than a warehouse or factory. This may be due to the fact unlike a factory full of machines, offices are more "homey" and easier to customize and personalize with our own symbols, behaviours and concrete artefacts of culture. There is furniture. There is food. There is the internet. There are photos of your family. It's like home. To a far greater degree than on the shop floor, 5S in the office threatens people's sense of personal space, and by extension their sense of self.

From the point of view of Concrete we need to understand the existing office culture in terms of the surface-level things such as furniture, equipment, files, food, and so forth. This is what most often gets 5S-ed; but we can't stop there. At the Behavioural level we need to understand how these things reflect on how people communicate, how groups of people are structured, their formal and tacit roles, and so forth. These things become more important determining factors in making change happen the higher up we go in the organization. Finally the Symbolic aspects of the office culture are very important and easy to miss. These are the real values and beliefs; how people see themselves, how they see others around them and how they see the work they do. At the simplest level this gets us back to guideline number one; do people have the will to improve, even excel or do they just work here?

The challenge with 5S in the office is to modify the Concrete aspects of culture in ways that also alter the Behavioural and Symbolic. Just as 5S makes process waste visible, whatever hides or enable the negative beliefs and values needs to be made visible through office 5S. That in the long-term is what makes office 5S work.

Chapter 8: Planning a 5S Office System

5S System, lean office, and Kaizen are popular terms used to describe a system used to find and remove all forms of waste in the work environment. These Kaizen principles that are used on shop floors around the world to increase productivity and efficiency can also be applied to the office environment. A 5S Office System will make your office clean, organized and office workers more efficient. Your office workers will be able to find what they need, when they need it and know exactly where everything is.

A 5S Office System will lay the foundation for a lean office that you can build on. Using the 5S System will make your office more productive, cleaner, raise office workers moral and save your company money. Once this lean office foundation is in place you can build on it using the principles of Kaizen to continuously improve your office environment and office management systems. The next few chapters will take you through the stages of planning and implementing a 5S Office System. The key to proper implementation of a 5S Office System is planning. Educate yourself on the 5S System and how it is used in the office.

Get The Support of Management

To be successful you will need the support of management and leadership. Prepare an overview of a what a 5S System is. Explain how it will make the workplace cleaner, more productive, more efficient, increase office worker moral and lower cost. Leadership likes to hear about low-cost ways to improve in these areas so these will be your key selling points.

Create a 5S Office Team

To help you plan and start a 5S Office System create a 5S Office Team. Team members will be managers, supervisors, team leads and your most organized and knowledgeable staff. Pick only a few relevant members of management. Most of the team should be office workers. The best feedback on improvement comes from those who actually do the work. They can tell you what works and what needs to be improved on. This team will help you plan and launch your 5S Office System as well as sustain it.

First Meeting

The goal of your first 5S Office System team meeting should be to educate your team members on the 5S System and to set the goals you want to achieve.

Discuss the 5S's
1. **Sort:** Remove everything from the office space that is not needed to do the work.
2. **Straighten:** A place for everything and everything in its place.
3. **Shine:** Cleanliness.
4. **Standardize:** Business rules to support the 5S System.

5. **Sustain:** Instil the self-discipline to sustain the 5S System.

Discuss the 7 Wastes in the Office
1. **Over Production:** More information than the customer needs, more information than the next process needs, creating reports no one reads, or making extra copies.
2. **Transportation:** Retrieving or storing files, carrying documents to and from shared equipment, taking files to another person, or going to get signatures.
3. **Motion:** Searching for files, extra clicks or keystrokes, clearing away files on the desk, gathering information, looking through manuals and catalogues, or handling paperwork.
4. **Waiting:** Waiting for faxes or a copy machine, for the system to come back up, for a customer response, or a handed-off file to come back.
5. **Unnecessary Processing:** Creating reports, repeated manual entry of data, use of outdated standard forms, or use of inappropriate software.
6. **Inventory:** Files waiting to be worked on, open projects, too many office supplies, e-mails waiting to be read, or unused records in the database.
7. **Defects:** Data entry errors, pricing errors, missing information, missed specifications, or lost records.

During this meeting you should set the goals for your 5S Office System. Examples of goals include:
1. Eliminate Waste.
2. Increase Productivity.
3. Increase Efficiency.
4. Better Organization.
5. Increase Your Office Workers Moral.
6. A Clean Work Environment.

Engage Your Office Workers

Before you launch meet with your office workers. During this meeting ask for as much feedback as you can get from them. They will have ideas you never thought of to help improve the office environment. Many of these can be integrated into the 5S Office System or used later as you build your lean office.

For a 5S Office System to work you must have everyone aboard. A 5S System is dependent on each office worker following the system and doing their part. You want to highlight that the office workers are the companies most valuable resource and that a 5S Office System will make their job easier.

Individual self-discipline will be required to sustain the system. By nature people are resistant to change so you should take a slow approach. It will make it easier to start and sustain the 5S System and have it accepted by office workers if they are part of the process.

Chapter 9: Laying the Foundation for 5S Office System

In the previous chapter we looked at the planning and first meeting stages of implementing a 5S Office System. Now you will learn how to build on this to lay the foundation for your 5S Office System.

First a word about overdoing it. The 5S system was created for the manufacturing environment. Part of this is using items such as shadow boards where the outline of a tool is placed on a peg board so you know where it goes and if it is missing. While I see great benefit for this in that environment, I have seen this translated to what I feel is an extreme in the office environment. Some 5S Office Systems will have you literally label each desk such as "stapler" and that is where your stapler must go. You may want to carry your system this far, but remember the goal of a 5S Office System is to create a more productive workplace and as a benefit to raise moral. Personally having my desk labelled with the locations of everything on it and being expected to keep it that way is extreme.

I do recommend standards for cleanliness and organization for desks and cubicles. The goal for the end of the day should be to have a desk that is clear and ready to start the next day. In my opinion, to actually label a desk and force workers to maintain that layout takes away the ability for each worker to adjust their workspace to fit their work flow.

Do you really want your 5S Office team to become office police going around taking away points because a stapler is not in its labelled position?

During Follow-Up Meetings

Once you have educated your 5S Office team and established the goals you want to accomplish it is time to plan your 5S Office System. Hold follow-up meetings to develop the tools and lay the foundation of your 5S Office System. Since the goal of the first 5S step is to remove all unnecessary items, your group must determine where everything goes. Create a map and log to indicate where everything will be located at the end of the campaign. Consider placing a 5S bulletin board in the office. On it you will place educational material about 5S and a map showing where everything is located. It is also an excellent location to place a suggestion box. You may be surprised at the good suggestions that can come from those who actually do the work.

Zone Mapping

A key benefit of a 5S Office System is being able to find what you need, when you need it and knowing where everything is. Tools to help you reach this goal will include maps and lists that can be posted around the office and on your company intranet. To help you determine what goes where take the office space and divide it into zones on an office map such as A1, B2, etc. If the office space is large and contains several different departments create a map specific for each department. Map the location of every filing cabinet either by what the contents are or by a letter or numbered system. Log these to a sheet which can be posted with the location map.

Desks and offices should be mapped not according to who is located there, but using a logical zone based system. For instance office C12 and desk B19. Your location map can easily show where office C12 and desk B19 is located. You can then create a separate document placing it on your company intranet to indicate who is in office C12 and at desk B19. Office equipment should also be zone based such as PA4 for the printer located in zone A4. As workers change locations and new workers are hired it is much easier and faster to accommodate their change of location using zone mapping. If someone is promoted from office C12 to office A3 the reference sheet can be easily updated. Inventory tracking is made easier because you can move the PC belonging to the worker in office C12 to office A3 and map them to the printer in zone A with a quick update.

Other benefits of mapping out your office is for your new team members. They can be given a map and reference sheet. They will then easily know where everything and everyone is located. It will also benefit groups such as the IT department. They will be able to track the inventory and location of every piece of equipment. For instance they can change printer names to match zone locations. When someone calls and says that printer PA4 is not working, they will know exactly where that is. Be sure to label office equipment for ease of identification.

Plan the Work Flow

One of the goals of a 5S campaign in the office is to improve efficiency and productivity. To enhance this consider the office layout and environment. Place filing cabinets containing designated documents close to those who use them the most. You should have a designated area for office supplies and cleaning supplies. If you do not have these consider building two closets for these items centrally located if possible. Consider the location of printers, fax machines, document shredders and other office equipment. How much time is wasted going to retrieve documents from a printer located on the far side of the room? Consider moving such items to a central location, near those who use them the most.

Since space in an office is valuable real estate look at the layout of desks, cabinets and office equipment. Walking through a maze or areas that are too close together is a waste of time and often hazardous. You want walkways to be clear of clutter and the office easy to navigate in. If there are pieces of office furniture or office equipment that is not needed, dispose of it or move it to a location that is out of the way.

Upgrade Your Office

Since the goal is to increase efficiency and productivity consider replacing any worn out office furniture and equipment. How much time is wasted dealing with that old printer? Consider replacing it with a modern multi-function printer.

All upgrades do not mean spending money. One way to save money is to go to a paperless office where possible. It reduces printing costs and the need for so many filing cabinets. You can scan documents into a portable format such as PDF and place them on a central and organized location on your company network. Access can be controlled with folder rights so only those who need access to the documents can get to them. Workers will never have to leave their desk to retrieve a document and documents will never be lost or out of place.

Upgrading the office environment can also increase efficiency and productivity by increasing worker moral. Workers who are happier about their work environment are more productive. Replacing worn out office furniture and office equipment, implementing better office organization and making it easier for workers to do their job can do wonders for increasing moral. Consider placing some pictures on those blanks walls. Plants and other office friendly decorations can liven up the work environment. If you have a break room look at upgrading it as well.

Designate Sort Zones

A lot of items will be out of place. To prepare for this you must designate three specific areas and provide plenty of boxes and bags to handle them all.

1. A place for items that need to be discarded. These are items you designate are no longer needed and can be thrown away. Be sure you have an area for

sensitive documents and a shredder to destroy them before disposal.

2. A place for items that are out of place. Before beginning a 5S sort campaign for the office you need to determine what goes where.

3. A place for items that have no designated area, but cannot be discarded. You will have to identify if you really need these items and if so where you will put them. Despite your best efforts for planning, there will always be pieces that you do not have an assigned place for.

5S Campaign Supplies

Be sure you have enough cleaning supplies for the shine step. Cleaning rags, cleaning solutions, brooms, dust pans, garbage bags and any other items that will be needed. You will need to have LOTS of boxes to hold items that are out of place. The last part of the Sort step will be to go through these boxes and tagged items and determine their fate.

Tags, labels and label makers will be very useful. During the 5S sort step items can be tagged to indicate where they came from and in which of the three designated sort zones they belong. Filing cabinets will need to be marked, as well as the folders inside them. Everything should be labelled for easy identification.

Chapter 10: Your First 5S Office Campaign

There are many benefits to a 5S Office System. Saving time, saving money, increasing efficiency, increasing production and increasing moral are just some examples.

In the previous chapter we looked at laying down the foundation of a 5S Office System. Now we will look to put everything to use by launching your first 5S Office Campaign.

By this time you should have all of your planning done and all of the supplies you need to support your 5S Office System.

1. A zone map designating where everything is located.
2. Designated sort areas for sorting items that are out of place or their status is unknown.
3. Supplies such as tags, boxes, trash bags, cleaning supplies.
4. Your office flow examined and a list of changes to be made.
5. Equipment and office furniture to be upgraded.

At this point you need to or should have already set the date of your first 5S Office campaign. Friday is always a good day to hold one on. Allow your team members to wear jeans and comfortable shoes. Most likely you will not be able to shut down office operations so plan your campaign in stages with as little interruption to team members as possible.

Set

Now it is time to bring the entire office staff onboard with the 5S Office System. Hold one large or several small meetings to educate them on what a 5S Office System is, what it means to them and how they will participate. It is a good idea to have hand-outs ready that explains the 5S Office System and what team members are expected to do. You will have lots of questions and a few grumbles, but as with anything that is new be patient as it will take time for everyone to get onboard.

By this time you should have all of the support structure in place. Zone maps should be posted around the office or on your organizations Intranet. If you plan on using a bulletin board it should already be up, along with a suggestion box.

The day before your campaign review everything with your 5S Office team. Be sure everyone knows their tasks and that everything is in place. You can expect plenty of bumps and forgotten items to show up so you should expect these. If your office is in really bad shape you may not get everything done in one day. For instance if you are upgrading equipment and furniture it would be best to do that after the first campaign is complete.

The goal of the first campaign is to clear out everything that does not belong and set everything in its place. This is the foundation you will build on. It may take several campaigns and be followed by daily, weekly and monthly work to get the 5S Office System in place and part of the daily routine.

Days or even weeks before you start your first campaign take pictures. You will post them on the 5S Office System bulletin board or Intranet web site as before and after pictures. They will serve as excellent reminders of how bad it was and how much better it is with a 5S Office System.

Go!

Launch day is here and your team is ready to go. Use the steps in the 5S Office System as your guide to run your campaign.

Sort

The Sort step for the office is about removing anything that is not necessary to do the work.

Sort through work areas and remove any unnecessary items such as books, supplies and files. Check inside all drawers, cabinets and storage areas.

The goal of the sort step is to remove anything that does not belong. Items that are out of place and items that a team member does not know where it goes should be taken to the designated sort areas. In the sort areas items should be tagged according to what is to be done with them. Relocation to a specific area and trash are the most likely outcomes. If in doubt, move it out. You can always come back and replace something if it is needed.

Each team member should be responsible for their own desk. You do not want members of your 5S Office team going through team members desk, cabinets or belongings. Give each employee at least one box to place items that do not belong in their work area. 5S Office team members can then take the boxes to the sort areas.

This is also the time to shred documents or other material that is no longer needed. You can create a lot of free space by getting rid of paperwork that is no longer needed. It will also make it easier in the next step when you organize and label all of your files and cabinets.

Straighten

Once all of the clutter has been removed it is time to put things in their place. Start by clearing out your sort areas and putting items where they belong. Next move through the office looking for anything that may have been missed. You want as much removed as possible to make the Shine step easier. Some items may have to wait until the Shine step has been completed to return them.

Arrange items so that they are easily accessible. Use a labelling system to label all folders and other items so they can be easily spotted. The goal is to be able to find what you are looking for in 30 seconds or less.

The motto for the Straighten step is "Everything has a place, everything in its place". This is your goal for this step. For most desks and cabinets this will just mean sorting through what is left and organizing it. If desks, furniture or equipment is to be moved to improve work flow this is the time to do it.

Shine

Now that all of the clutter has been removed and everything has been put in to place it is time to clean. This is the step where people will really start to notice the results.

Clean everything in the work area including all office equipment. If your office equipment has not been recently serviced, service it yourself or setup a service call. Move furniture if needed to get everything swept or vacuumed. Literally look high and low for dirt, trash and gunk. You will be surprised at what you will find.

Standardize

The last two steps are about installing a system that will support and maintain the 5S Office System. You should already have written a document explaining to everyone what is expected of them. Detail what should be done at the end of each day, each week and each month.

Establish standards for how the work areas should be maintained. Everything should be kept clean and organized. When items are pulled for use they should be returned when you are done with them. Standardization is important to maintaining and improving on the system.

At the end of each workday you want each work area to be ready to start work the next day. Don't allow files and paperwork to pile up on desks. They should be disposed of or returned to where they belong when they are no longer needed. This should be part of the daily routine and should become a habit for everyone.

Sustain

Be sure that everyone is following the new 5S Office System standards. This is about making sure everyone is following the 5S Office System and doing their part. A word of warning here. You do not want to establish a 5S Office police force. A negative opinion will develop very quickly. You want everyone to be onboard and it may take others longer to get with the new system. Be patient!

If your first 5S Office campaign was done properly everyone should notice the difference. Being able to find what you need when you need it, not having to walk halfway across the building to get office supplies, seeing the office clean and tidy should raise moral. The goal of the Sustain step is to instil a philosophy that will make the 5S Office system part of the office culture.

Evaluation

Now that your first 5S Office campaign is complete it is time to meet with your 5S team members and see what worked and what needs to be improved on. Don't expect everything to go perfect the first time. Your 5S Office System should include continuous improvement. Things will change and your system must adapt to those changes.

If you did not get everything done this time make plans for your next campaign. If your plan includes replacing old equipment or office furniture make plans to do this now. You probably ran across things you did not plan for or uncovered things you did not know existed.

The most effective system is one where everyone takes 15 minutes at the end of each day to perform the first three steps. If they make 5S part of their daily routine it should take less time than this. This also gives them time to set themselves up so they can start work with a clean slate the next day.

If needed set aside more time at the end of the day on Friday to perform the first three steps in more detail than can be done during the week. Having everything sorted, back in its place and cleaned makes Monday mornings a lot more tolerable and productive.

Plan on having monthly 5S Office campaigns on set dates. The last Friday of the month is a good time. Make it an event that people will look forward to rather than dread. Bring in snacks, make it a casual

Friday, be creative to make it not only productive in maintaining the 5S Office System, but a moral booster as well. You may want to put a little competition into it by rewarding people or teams with the best areas. Gift cards or other rewards are a good incentive.

Most of all remember that a 5S Office System is about making the workplace better. More efficient, more productive, cleaner and raising moral. It is not a rigid system that must be followed "or else". You want your 5S Office System to be accepted and work. This will lay the foundation for further improvements in the future. A successful 5S Office System that is accepted and followed will make it much easier to make these improvements in the future.

Chapter 11: Sustaining the 5S Office System

5S System Standardize and Sustain are the fourth and fifth steps in a 5S Office System. These last two steps are about keeping your 5S Office System running smoothly. To do this you must set up standards and reinforce the 5S Office System.

After the last chapter "Your First 5S Office Campaign" you now have your 5S Office System in place. Now we will look at how you can sustain and improve the system over time.

Establish Standards

To make sure the 5S Office System is followed you must set up standards. The goal is to put to paper standards for how you want your office workspace to be maintained. These are the rules but don't call them that, call them standards.

Here is an example of standards for conference rooms
1. No food is allowed in the conference room.
2. Doors should be closed during all meetings.
3. Cell phones should be put on silent before a meeting starts.
4. White boards must be cleared at the end of the meeting.

5. All chairs must be put back in place and if extra seating is brought in it must be removed at the end of the meeting.
6. The meeting organizer is responsible for making sure the conference room is clean and returned to standards at the end of each meeting. (accountability).

Remember a 5S Office System is more than keeping things clean and organized. It should include office etiquette as well. You are changing the culture of the office so this must include a code of behaviour such as turning off cell phones before a meeting starts.

Standards should be established for every common workspace and personal workspace. How they should be laid out, how they should be labelled, how they should be organized, and how they should be maintained.

Other areas to consider:
1. How desks and offices should be maintained.
2. How filing cabinets and common work areas should be maintained.
3. When files are pulled they must be returned to the proper filing cabinet by the end of each day.
4. Common work areas must be kept clean and organized.
5. At the end of each day desks should be cleared and ready for work the next day.

Don't become a 5S Czar by laying down rules that are so rigid people will not follow them. Standards should be best practices for maintaining a clean, organized and productive work environment. Standards are the who, what, when, where and how of your 5S Office System.

Sustain the 5S Office System

The fifth and last step in a 5S Office System is the sustain step. With the sustain step you want to instil the self-discipline needed for everyone to follow the 5S Office System. You also want to lay the groundwork for changing the office culture.

Reinforce Your 5S Office Team

Continue to hold regular meetings with your 5S Office team to check the system. 5S utilizes Kaizen which is a philosophy of small, but continuous improvements. No matter how good your system is it can always be improved.

Evaluate your system to see if your goals are being met and if new goals need to be added. Look at areas where the system is not working well and find out why. These meetings should cover the 5S Office System as well as the office culture.

Reinforce Your Employees

Old habits die hard over and over time the newness of the 5S Office System will wear off and some people will be tempted to return to their old habits. The sustain step will make sure this does not happen.

By nature people are resistant to change and others may think this is just another fad that will fade away.

One way to reinforce your employees is to hold monthly 5S Office campaigns. Over time slippage will occur and more extensive sort, straighten and shine steps will need to be carried out. As with your first campaign make it an office event. Make it a jeans Friday and bring in snacks.

Hold a meeting or have a lunch to get feedback from employees. The goal is to keep employees engaged in the 5S Office System so they know it is not going to fade away. Only then will it become a habit and part of the office culture.

Contests are often used in 5S Systems. Rewards are good incentives and the benefits you reap will be well worth the cost. The contests can be the best example of a 5S Office workspace, and awards for teams or departments. It will raise moral and yield better results than disciplinary actions.

Three Keys to Success

1. Ensure everyone knows what is expected of them. How can you expect people to follow a system they do not understand or is not clearly defined by standards?

2. Set aside a specific time of day to carry out the sort, straighten and shine steps. This is the biggest key to success. You must give your employees the time to support the system. Those 10-15 minutes at the end

of each day are likely already lost with people preparing to go home. Utilize this time to support the system. You want this to become a habit and habits are formed by repetition.

3. Reinforce both your 5S Office team and your employees to keep the 5S Office system from fading away.

Chapter 12: Continuous Improvement of a 5S System

No system remains perfect. The workplace and workspaces change. The work being done changes. For whatever reason a 5S System must always be improved upon. You should regularly review your 5S System and look for ways to improve it. Have a meeting before each monthly 5S event to discuss and get feedback for improvement from employees.

Continuous Improvement is the on-going effort to improve products, services and processes by making small, incremental improvements within a business. It is based on the belief that these incremental changes will add up to major improvements over time and it is as much about tactics (i.e. specific improvements) as it is about changing the culture of the organization to focus on opportunities for improvement rather than problems.

Here are four factors that are essential to successful continuous improvement programs:

1. Leadership that walks the talk

The support of an organization's leadership team is usually cited as the number one factor for the success of a continuous improvement initiative. Leaders must exhibit behaviours that not only demonstrate support for the initiative but also the behaviours that they wish all employees to emulate. This ultimately comes down to guidance and the support within the organisation to make the change. If there is not adequate support for a continuous improvement program to be implemented, then the team charged with implementing it will be operating on what will be, in effect, a series of isolated efforts.

2. A focus on "fire prevention" rather than "fire fighting"

No individual, team or company can implement change if they don't have the time or mental capacity to do so. The trouble is that often it is often the very problems that need fixing that are creating a series of "fires" that constantly distract managers from solving the root cause of their problems. Everyone is constantly having to work harder, rather than smarter. Worse, some company cultures celebrate and reward those employees and managers who put out the most fires, which removes incentive to prevent the fires in the first place.

3. Constancy of purpose

In Dr. W. Edwards Deming's "14 points" he called for the "constancy of purpose for continual improvement of products and service to society." This unrelenting, unwavering focus on improvement is critical to maintaining and sustaining process improvements in the long term. Changes need to maintain momentum to ensure the changes are not forgotten and don't grind to a halt through fatigue or resistance. Successful continuous improvement programs understand that improvement is not merely a management initiative; a so-called "flavour of the month" but a long-term practice that needs to permeate everything an organization does.

4. Shift to long term mind-set

Managers are often focused on whether they are going to meet their monthly or quarterly targets and it can be very difficult to prioritize improvements that will only make an impact over the longer term. As a result, continuous improvement is as much about mind-set as it is about actions. The company needs to start looking at the long-term impact of the work it is doing and understand that a quarterly dip in performance can be tolerated if it means that in the long term, the company is in a better position both financially and in terms of the company's ability to deliver outstanding products and services to its customers.

The clue to successful continuous improvement is in the name. It must be continuous so that opportunities for growth can be highlighted, improvement made and measured and evaluated.

Chapter 13: Benefits of 5S in the Office

Why should I care about 5S in the office?

Sort, Set in order, Shine, Standardize and Sustain, these are the famous 5S that people talk about. 5S has been a tool that have been normally used in the manufacturing environment and for this same reason when companies try to implement 5S in the office, they face a lot of resistance from the office workers. I normally hear people saying : "this is for the shop floor at the office we do thinks different". What people normally miss is the purpose of doing 5S.

The purpose of 5s is to make problems and opportunities for improvement visible, such as: excessive time looking for files, tools, papers, safety issues, excessive office supplies etc.

These are other benefits of using a 5s program in your office, shop or home:
1. You can't work to the best of your abilities when your office is a disorganized mess.
2. Your workspace is a visual representation of what kind of person you are; that is how your clients and supervisors see it.
3. Out-of-control office clutter costs money in time, effort, late fees and lost business.
4. 5S helps you get rid of things that take up space, even stuff you think you might need "someday."

5. Sort through and reduce piles of paper by using a four-box sorting system.
6. 5S helps you avoid daunting heaps of paper, put things right back after you use them.
7. The discipline of 5S allows you to organize materials for the next day before leaving your office. So the next day you are set to go.
8. 5S enable yourself to find what you want when you want it.

The Advantages of Implementing a 5S System

In order to participate in the global economy and compete against companies that are advantaged by overseas production, businesses are looking to find ways to reduce cost, improve quality and increase productivity. For this reason, businesses are implementing lean manufacturing, which allows for improvements in productivity while increasing the quality of the output. Lean manufacturing systems use minimal amounts of resources to produce high volume of high-quality goods with some variety, allowing companies to make better use of available resources.

The 5S process is one of the most fundamental and widely applied components of lean manufacturing. Its application is simple, involving basic common sense; however, the advantages cannot be underestimated due to its simplicity. Once implemented a 5s system can be the stabilizing force underlying a lean manufacturing strategy.

As we know; the 5s system derives its name from the five Japanese words which define the process, they are: seiri, seiton, seiso, seiketsu and shitsuke. Translated into English they are: sort, set in order, shine, standardize and sustain.

The guiding principles underlying the 5S system involve organization, cleanliness and standardization. Overall workplace cleanliness, created by removing waste from the work area, promotes internal organization and enhances visual communication. By reducing wasted time and materials, productivity is increased along with safety and costs are reduced.

The following is a list of the most obvious benefits which can be derived from implementation of the 5s system.

1. Increases in productivity:
   a. Reduces lead times thereby improving product delivery times.
   b. Reduces equipment downtime, maintenance and cycle time.
   c. Improves daily and shift start-up times and reduces changeover time.
   d. Reduces the amount of time wasted searching for tools and equipment.

2. Increases in quality:
   a. Improves quality by reducing the amount of errors/defects.
   b. Implements standardization there by achieving output consistency.
   c. The pleasantries of the simplified work environment increases employee moral

73

3. Reduction in cost:

   a. Provides cost-savings by reducing inventory, storage fees and space requirements.

   b. Improves safety thereby reducing the cost of worker injuries.

   c. Reduces the amount of scrap thereby reducing production cost.

   d. The system as a whole minimizes waste and improves efficiency by ensuring that workers are spending time doing productive task rather than looking for misplaced tools, sorting unnecessary through stacks of waste material or rearranging the work environment at the change of shifts.

One of the great aspects of implementing a 5s system is that it can be done today and everyone can participate. Furthermore, all businesses and all departments can benefit from the 5s system.

Manufacturing and industrial plants have the greatest applications; however, its use is not limited to production areas. Office and administration areas, information or data flow hubs, retail space and service delivery systems can also achieve productivity gains from its implementation. The bottom line advantage to any company is an increase in profits and a maximization of shareholder wealth.

Chapter 14: How Your Business Can Benefit from 5S Principles

Whenever I have come across an examples of where 5S principles have been applied, there is almost always two images displayed depicting a "before" and "after" image of a typical section of an office, warehouse, factory or piece of a machinery. Invariably, the "before" picture shows a grimy, dirty state of affairs and the "after " picture as if by some bit of magic shows the same item now cleaned and looking bright and shiny. The problem with this portrayal is it only demonstrates one aspect of the 5S – the cleaning.

Let's start at the beginning. What is 5S? Very simply, this is a way of working (a methodology) used initially to organise workplaces to be more efficient and streamlined thereby consistently striving for more outputs, lower costs and less waste. So in essence, as this is what Continuous Improvement is mostly about, 5S is one of the commonly used Continuous Improvement tools.

The recommended way to adopt and live 5S should be to approach it as a journey rather than a destination. Once you reach the standardise stage, it can be quite easy for standards to slip back to old ways, hence the sustaining stage should go on for as long as necessary up until it has been embedded as part of a new culture; therefore we recommend that you make 5S a key part of your Continuous

Improvement machinery, regardless of the type of business you are in.

Prioritise conducting 5S in workplaces where the efficiency improvement would benefit the business most, especially where there is a customer impact or interface. For example it's more essential to do a 5S in the order processing office rather than the staff coffee making machine area.

Stating the overall intention and anticipated benefits will add weight to every 5S initiative. Consider linking it to some tangible benefit such as; by conducting 5S we aim to reduce our customer waiting time from the current 10 minutes to about 5 minutes.

Create a team building atmosphere and conduct 5S in teams rather than as individuals. This allows a common approach, making the standardisation stage more representative and giving it a greater chance to succeed.

There is normally no need to go out of your way and spend loads of money on 5S. Basic discipline and common sense is mostly what is required.

5S principles go beyond the office, consider using the 5S in today's increasingly information technology driven environments for the efficient storage, protection retrieval and maintenance of data and files.

Chapter 15: 5S for the Email Inbox

Every email is a decision waiting to be made.

The average individual sends/receives 125 emails a day. That's 600+ per week. No wonder companies are concerned with overloaded and at-capacity servers. Your email Inbox is one of the easiest places to have clutter in your office because only you and Mr. IT know what is hiding there.

Using the 5S technique to better manage your email Inbox breaks down into these five steps.

1. Sort: If your email management program offers a "rules" feature, decide which emails can be pre-sorted into folders so they don't even end up in your Inbox. Think about non-time sensitive emails such as HR notices, Professional Association newsletters, notifications from social media, and announcements from vendors such as airlines, hotels and department stores. You will feel more in-control knowing that these items are no longer allowed to interrupt your focus with non-urgent business.

2. Straighten: Set up a file folder structure that mirrors the project folders sitting on your desk. For example, if you are working on a project called Jones's Product create a project folder on your desk with that label and then create an email file folder to hold emails related to it. Finally, go one step further and create a file with the same name on your computer. Filing an email and retrieving it later will be much easier if you have carefully chosen the proper name of your folders. Avoid creating too many file folders which will only dissuade you in the future from using them and encourages you to leave emails in your Inbox.

3. Sweep or Shine: Once a week go through your Inbox and delete the emails that are no longer needed. It is estimated that 50% of read email can be deleted once read. If an email represents a future action, create a task for it, removing it from your Inbox. If you use MS® Outlook you can drag your email to your Tasks and create a separate task, keeping the email's content with it. If it is something related to a future appointment, insert the email or drag it to your calendar.

4. Standardize: For Outlook users, did you know you can colour-code emails coming into your Inbox? You can even colour code emails sent only to you (no one else who was cc'd or bcc'd on it). I recently met someone who even colour codes the emails coming from her boss! Here is how to do that within Outlook:

    a. Once an email arrives in your inbox, highlight it without opening it.
    b. Click on Tools > Organize.
    c. Click on "Using Colours" in the menu that opens up and assign a colour.
    d. This is also the area where you can specify colours of emails sent only to you.

Be careful not to go overboard with colour coding. A few strategic colours can definitely guide your eye in recognizing email from key people.

5. Sustain: Maintenance doesn't happen automatically. Giving your Inbox attention must occur on a regular basis. Allow yourself time each Friday afternoon to apply these 5S techniques to your Inbox. It is such a great feeling returning to your office on Monday morning, knowing your Inbox isn't filled with unnecessary clutter.

Chapter 16: 5S for Filing Systems

When it comes to being disorganized, is it any surprise that paper continues to be one of the biggest problems that plague people at home and at the office? Before organizing (and hopefully filing) those piles of paper sitting on your desk, you have got to get your existing filing cabinets ready. Even if your current filing system isn't bursting at the seams, it will still be a good idea to sort through and remove any unnecessary papers in order to make room for future storage needs. Just a quick reminder that 5S is a systematic approach to keeping an area neat and organized. Originally designed by Toyota, it is now adapted by industries world-wide in both manufacturing and offices settings.

Applying the 5S technique to your filling system breaks down into these 5 usual manageable steps:

1. Sort: Slow and steady is your mantra when doing this step. Start at the front of your drawer and begin to sort through, one file at a time. This might seem too time-consuming for you so use a timer and limit your session to just 15-20 minutes a day. Slow and Steady progress will prevent any type of burn-out, especially if you are facing a lot of files. Use a brightly coloured piece of paper as a marker in your file drawer so you know where to pick up the next day.

2. Straighten: If your filing cabinet has hanging file folders, chances are you have plastic tabs identifying the file name. Reposition these tabs so they are directly behind one another vs. having them in any type of staggered positioning. Referred to as Straight-line Filing, this actually allows you to find a folder more quickly.

3. Sweep or Shine: Take time to "clean-up" as you go. If you have got files with broken tabs, replace them now. If some of your manila file folders are tattered or just plain worn out, replace with a new supply that is crisp-looking. (If you use Manila file folders inside hanging files, use Interior Manila file folders as they are designed to completely nest inside a hanging file without sticking up. This makes for a very neat-looking file drawer.)

4. Standardize: Be consistent in how you label your individual files and file drawers. If you have got a label maker it will be much easier to create that "standardized" look. Also, file only what is absolutely necessary. If you have the document electronically, do you still need to make a copy for your filing cabinet?

5. Sustain: Keeping your filing cabinet neat, orderly and easy-accessible is the name of the game moving forward. If your filing system is quite extensive, create a File Index in Excel which will allow easy updates. Print this Index and hang it on a clipboard on the side of your filing cabinet so you (and others) can easily reference it when filing items. Keep a supply of 8-10 empty hanging files and Manila file folders in the front of your filing cabinet. This way you will have what you need at your fingertips the next time you need to create a new file.

Chapter 17: Improving Your Office Environment

You might be an organized individual but there is a difference between being organized and being clean. Believe it or not, you can have one without the other, however it is optimum when they are combined.

As Toyota refined their Lean Manufacturing methodology they paid close attention to the maintenance of their assembly line equipment. In time they saw the number of breakdowns decrease but also the cost to repair a breakdown decrease as well.

In offices today cleaning crews are scheduled to come in at night to empty garbage cans, vacuum the floors and clean the bathrooms. They do not, however, pay close attention to the amount of dust collecting on the top of your filing cabinet, the dust bunnies living amidst your computer cables, or the dirt collecting on "stuff" piled throughout your office. They also completely tune out the layers of sticky notes lining the perimeter of your computer screen or bulletin board.

In the Sweep category a clean space consistently insures quality and efficiency. The catch phrase often used for the Sweep step of 5S is "The best cleaning is to not need cleaning." I wish my teenage son could grasp this concept for his bedroom.

Here is your challenge: Take two minutes – that is only 120 seconds and do one of the following items. You will probably love the outcome so much that you will take additional time to tackle more.

1. Wipe down all flat surfaces with a damp paper towel or anti-bacterial cloth. Studies have proven that there are 400 times more bacteria on your desk and phone than on a toilet seat.

2. Remove programs on your computer that you never use. To view a list of existing programs, click on the Start button > Control Panel > Programs > Uninstall a Program. If you are unsure of what a program does, speak with someone in your IT department before removing it from your machine.

3. De-clutter your computer desktop. Review the icons and shortcuts on your computer screen. Remove those that you no longer need/use. For the remaining icons, arrange them on your computer desktop so you can easily find what you are looking for i.e. Cluster Word documents in one corner while arranging spreadsheets or PowerPoint presentations in another corner.

4. If you have plants in your office make sure they are healthy ones. Wipe off dusty leaves with a damp cloth, remove dead leaves, stems and check for mouldy soil and leaves.

5. Dust/wipe off picture frames, knick-knacks or other items that gather dust but are rarely cleaned.

6. Using a can of air or a product like Cyber Clean, clean your keyboard and the touchpad of your phone, fax machine and cell phone.

If you need a little motivation, ask yourself if you are "tour ready". At any given moment, would you be proud to show your office to your customers or vendors? Perhaps a little cleaning is in order.

Chapter 18: Running In-house 5S Training Course

This chapter will look at how to run an in-house 5S training course, what the specific steps should be and what should be covered and how. We will also recommend the different materials that you may need to be able to gain the best results possible from your trainees.

Before you start your 5S in-house training course.

Any 5S implementation program should follow and build on the overall aims of the business, you need to ensure that what you are trying to achieve with 5S both follows the strategy of your business. Familiarize yourself with the business objectives and create a small presentation as to how 5S can help the company to achieve those aims and the benefits of 5S, it is important that the trainees are fully aware that what they are doing will impact the overall performance and future of the company.

Select the area in which you wish to start your 5S implementation program and also select the people that you wish to have in your 5S team, they should mainly be people from the area in which you will apply 5S but feel free to add a few people from areas in which 5S will be implemented in the near future including implementing 5S for the office.

If there are no measures of performance in place for the area in which you are going to conduct your 5S training or if they are not suitable; define and begin to gather data for your 5S performance measures. These results will form a baseline against which any improvement will be measured. Involve the manager and supervisor at this stage to get their buy in and help in developing and recording this data.

Take as many photographs of the area and processes as possible to become a visual baseline for your improvements.

5S In-house Training course format

My suggestions would be to use a variety of different medias in conducting your training to ensure that as many people as possible get as much information as they can. Everyone learns in different ways so the more variety you can introduce into your 5S in-house training course the better.

5S Training Introduction

This is where a short presentation regarding the aims of the company and of this specific implementation should be given, if possible have this introduction given by the CEO or another respected member of senior management to show their support for the initiative.

Train in identifying the Seven Wastes

The seven wastes are an important aspect of any 5S program, after all you will be trying to eliminate these wastes within your processes. This presentation should cover what they are along with some examples. You should also cover the basics of lean manufacturing and the benefits of lean manufacturing; no more than 10 minutes for lean in general.

I would usually follow this up with a quick trip to the gemba (workplace) with pens and post-its to get the team to identify what they consider to be wasteful steps within their area; they should identify many wastes. Have them feedback the wastes to the team and use the post-its to organize them in a logical way. These can be used as a reference in later stages of 5S as you can attempt to eliminate or reduce them.

5S In-House Training

Now you should give them an overview of 5S, I normally (rather than put up many slides and talk for hours) start with a simple 5S simulation or game then a 5S DVD to run through the learning points within the game. This can be a fun introduction to 5S and will get the message over regarding what you are trying to achieve.

This should then be followed by a few slides to remind all what the first step of 5S is Seiri sort; and everyone should descend onto the workplace with the clear objective of removing all clutter from the workplace and using red tags and your quarantine area. Have a clear time limit after which you will regroup to review what has been done. As the trainer your job is to support all members of the team, challenge what they are leaving and what they are removing. This should continue until everyone is happy that all clutter is removed.

The second and third stages of 5S; 5S Seiton and 5S Seiso, should be presented with just a few slides as a reminder and once again the team should return to the workplace to begin organizing and cleaning everything there. Again have a clear time limit for each visit to the workplace and keep reviewing what people are doing and make suggestions and comparisons to the DVD etc. Also review the wastes identified earlier and see if actions undertaken have eliminated or reduced these wastes, if not try to tackle them within this stage.

If at any stage the team is starting to flounder or have nothing to do it is time to bring them back into the in-house training room and review what has been done and still needs to be done. Remember your role here is really one of facilitation, you need to allow the team to come up with the ideas for improvement not you force them onto them.

At the end of these three stages the team should create a list of actions to be conducted and any other recommendations or requests to continue the first three stages. These should be fed back to management to show what has been achieved and gain approval for any expenditure required; generally most improvements at this stage are not expensive, you will normally be looking at purchasing or manufacturing different racking styles and tooling holders and other minor changes.

Dates and responsibilities should be assigned to all of these actions and the team should plan to implement them at later stages at an agreed date; dependent on the work remaining to be done.

During this break; no more than 3 or 4 weeks, the employees should continue to apply what they have learned to make additional improvements and to implement the agreed actions.

The training should then recommence with a review of what has been achieved including a review of the previously agreed measures before moving onto the forth step of 5S that of 5S standardization or Seiketsu; during this portion of the training you should again present just a few slides and some examples of standardization. The team should then be split into relevant groups to begin defining standardized operations and instructions. This should only take one or two days depending on the size and complexity of the area in question.

At the end of this session I would suggest another break of around 2 weeks during which the team should continue to improve their area and the new standardized operating instructions.

Concluding your In-house 5S Training

The final stage of 5S (5S Shitsuke or sustain) should then be presented to the team after a review of what has happened and improved in the previous stages and weeks. This is often the hardest stage of the training especially if the senior management has not been seen to be fully supportive of the initiative in the previous weeks.

Create a 5S story board to publicize the benefits of the implementation of 5S, show before and after photographs as well as displaying the ongoing graphs for audits and the like.

Chapter 19: Office Kaizen

Kaizen means improvement. People often use the term when referring to the continuous improvement process. After concluding your In-house 5S Training you should organise series of kaizen to keep the 5S Office momentum alive. Suggesting and implementing kaizen on a regular basis should become part of the company's culture and system. In other words, it is standardized.

Office kaizen is essential to cost saving. Staff members should be asked to fill out two kaizen suggestion forms per month as part of their monthly reporting requirements. Managers should check the employees' suggestions. It is then management's responsibility to implement the suggestions or explain why they cannot be implemented. You should ensure that this managerial responsibility is also standardized.

It works because requirements and accountability are built into the system for both staff and managers. Employees can get quickly de-motivated and stop making kaizen suggestions if they feel their ideas are not being heard or respected.

Overheard in the office

"Kaizen implementation can be a hassle for me as a team leader. It requires extra effort. But, at the end of the day, it makes work more efficient for my staff and productivity goes up. We are continually cost saving." Team Leader, Toyota supplier, Japan.

Office Kaizen Implementation

Step 1: Implement a 5s Kaizen Program

A 5s office system is mandatory for the elimination of waste, workplace efficiency and cost saving. "It is the foundation of our success," says Office Manager of A Medical Device Company. Implement 5s Kaizen standards as part of your lean office strategy.

Step 2: Implement a standardized office kaizen system

A Creative Suggestion System that is focused on the elimination of waste. Some people may say that there is not a single item of work which is wasted. But the more we think about it, the more we become aware of many types of work which is unnecessary. Things change. In the past, there may have been a reason to do a particular job, but now there is no real reason.

An example of wasted work: An employee in an office had the responsibility to transcribe the contents of payment vouchers and receiving slips into a notebook. The worker said "I inherited this work from my predecessor. I have been on this job for two years and no one has ever asked to see the notebook. If I stop doing this work, I can save 20 hours each month." In suggesting that this work be eliminated, she also mentioned that all the chits were kept in the document room, and any necessary information could be obtained within 30 minutes. If the work had not been utilized for two years, there was certainly no justification for the continuation, especially when there was another way of finding the required information.

In most administrative divisions seldom does a division manager or section chief know how any one of his subordinates handles his day to day work. Ask a question to a division manager: "Can you find any waste in the routine work performed by your administrative employees?" The answer you receive is often "Well I haven`t really looked into the work of admin staff. I don`t know." Therefore it is important to ask each and every one of the workers to think about his or her own work routine. The manager`s function is to accept suggestions, coordinate them and see to that these kaizen suggestions are implemented. Small group activities, such as QC circles and QC groups can be effective at fostering employees willingness for participate in office kaizen activities.

Regarding Office Kaizen, ask the following questions.
1. Is there any work that is being done which is really not necessary?
2. Can the work procedure be simplified?
3. Is there a better way of doing it?
4. What will happen if we change or adjust our tools?

Management must then take the next logical step and bunch together the hours saved to make it possible for the division to withdraw a worker. To withdraw workers and do it thoroughly is one of the characteristics of the Toyota production system.

The Creative Suggestion System

It is important for each worker to submit a suggestion showing how his own work and the group`s work can be improved. In order to make this happen, it is vital to establish an atmosphere which is conducive to receiving suggestions. The next important consideration is for a superior to form the habit of listening to every suggestion presented to him. To be heard is more important to employees than to receive a $10 or $20 award for kaizen suggestions.

Chapter 20: Office 5S Tips

Some of the benefits of applying 5S to your work area is finding it easier to get things done, you will be more productive, have more time and feel more in control (less stress). The more you do 5S the better you get at it. Set aside one hour a day and get started.

Learn to ask "Why" (5 times if needed) to get to the root cause of problem. Then think of possible solutions to eliminate these problem. Try implementing solutions to these problem. An old 10 word two letter saying "If it is to be it is up to me". However don't work on targets alone; get one of your team members to help.

Think about your routine and the work you do. Think of the things that cause stress, interruptions, telephone calls, anything using your time, anything that feels like waste. There is at least 40% waste in most operations. Seek out and eliminate this waste.

Also remember the 80/20 rule. 80% of problems come from 20% of the causes (sometimes 80% of the problems come from only 2 or 3% of the causes). Remember usage determines location and storage; things you use often should be close and easily accessible.

Some ideas that may help your work flow.
1. Get someone else to look at your work area and make suggestions.

2. Rearrange your furniture; make it easy to get to things you use in your work.
3. Remove things in your work area you don't use.
4. Get more storage (files, etc) if needed.
5. Purge files periodically.
6. Do a filing system that works good for your area and keep it up.
7. Use a tickler system at your desk.
8. Use folders in internal email and Outlook for better organization.

More thoughts on office 5S

Look at trying to make improvements to your work area first. Why? We get immediate personal benefits. We have less stress and more time. With more time we can do more 5S activities.

Look for hidden 5S opportunities (opportunities is a nice way to say problems). Such as paper flow (why do we need paper?), procedures, policies (are they out of date and need to be revised\updated?).

Are there policies and procedures that we should be following and are not? Use 5S tools to help Standardize and Sustain them. You may need to use other tools to work on these problem.

Use tools such as the Theory of Constraints "TOC" 5 Step problem solving form.

A little input from TOC: Ely Goldratt, author of the book "The Goal", and originator of the Theory of

Constraints training often asks this question of his students, "What are you waiting for?"

You know how to identify waste and substandard performance. You have been trained on how to list the cause of constraints. You also know how to list cures and subordinate others to help. But, most of all, you know how good it feels to implement improvement and elevate a constraint. So...why do you wait?

Chapter 21: Conclusion

5S principles are as applicable in a service industry or your administrative offices as they are in Manufacturing; in fact in some cases even more important. Applying 5S tools to your office processes will often make greater savings in your lead times and other issues than you could ever hope to make on your production.

Consider most companies order processing; how many times have you observed a six weeks lead time being taken up with 5 weeks in the office and one week of panicked production? This is far from unusual unfortunately, so applying lean ideas and 5S tools has got to be a way forward.

Just as in our production areas, it is often best to have a 5S Program for our office areas, the principles and ideas are just the same with the same goals; an organized, safe, clean, efficient and repeatable work flow. Work to prevent the wastes of Muda, Mura and Muri and eliminate those seven wastes within your office.

5S in the office is as important, if not more so, than 5S in your production areas. A 5S System is a low cost system that will clean and organize your workplace. It will increase productivity and raise employee moral.

One of the keys to the success of a 5S system is to have the full support of the management of your company. While a 5S system is low cost to implement, it will require changes to the work habits of employees and needs the support and reinforcement of management.

Educate Yourself on 5S

The first thing you need to do is educate yourself on 5S. Write an overview of what the 5S system is and how it will be implemented in your company. Present your proposal to management for their approval.

You may meet resistance since old habits are hard to break. Explain how the 5S system is a useful tool that can improve productivity, promote safety and lower costs. Explain how the 5S system will make the workplace cleaner, safer and more pleasant for the employees. Emphasize the low cost involved to implement and the potential savings of a successful 5S system. Management loves to hear of low cost ways to save the company money.

Create a 5S System Plan and a 5S Team

Before you begin a 5S System you must plan for it. This involves walking around the workplace and taking notes. Look at how people work. How far away is the work to be done and the tools and parts used to do the work from the workstation? What is lying around that is not used? Are there any obvious work hazards? If so they should be taken care of immediately. Explore every area, every file cabinet, every drawer looking for items that do not belong where they are. From these notes you can map out your plan of attack.

A 5S system is a team concept. It requires the participation of everyone in order to sustain it. You should pick a core group of people from various workstations to be members of your 5S team. 5S team members should be well organized and with a good sense for the workflow. While long-term employees are valuable members, someone who has not been around long can add a set of "fresh eyes" to team. Once your team is intact you need to hold a series of planning sessions.

As you did with management, the first step with your 5S team will be to educate them on what 5S is and the benefits of it. During these sessions you need to determine how the 5S system will be implemented in your workplace. There is no one size fits all approach, but each step of the 5S system should be implemented, monitored and continuously improved.

The Steps of 5S for the Office

The same 5 steps of 5S that you applied in your manufacturing areas are applicable within your administrative processes. Just as within your production processes you must start with training and the team should be formed by mainly those people who work in the area in which you are conducting 5S.

Some tools that may help you with your 5S System include:
1. Educational materials for the 5S team and employees. Posters placed around the workplace will remind employees of the 5S System.

2. A bulletin board dedicated to the 5S System. You can post educational material, event notices and location charts of designated areas. Before and after pictures are very useful to show how bad things were and how much better they are now.

3. Rewards such as recognition of areas, groups or teams for their efforts in support of the 5S System.

5S is a team oriented system, allow anyone to offer suggestions on improvements. You will be surprised at what employees can come up with. Plus, no one knows better how the work flows than the ones doing the work.

Good luck !!